Why Are So Many Black Folks In Jails?

The Conspiracy to Exterminate Blacks, Colored Folks, African Americans and Negroids in 21st Century America

The Collateral Consequences of Saying Nothing, Doing Nothing and Allowing The United States Government, Politicians and the Judicial System To Go Unchecked.

Dr. Tracy Andrus

Table of Contents

The Facts

According to the Bureau of Justice Statistics 2009;

- In 2009, over **7.2 million** people were on probation, in jail or prison, or on parole at yearend — 3.1% of all U.S. adult residents or **1 in every 32 adults**. The total correctional population declined (down 0.7% or 48,800 offenders) during 2009, the first decline observed in the population since the Bureau of Justice Statistics began reporting this population in 1980.

- At yearend 2009 a total of **4,203,967** adult men and women were on probation and **819,308** were on parole or mandatory conditional release following a prison term.

- State and federal prison authorities had jurisdiction over **1,613,740** prisoners at yearend 2009: **1,405,622** under state jurisdiction and **208,118** under federal jurisdiction.

- Local jails held **760,400** adults awaiting trial or serving a sentence at midyear 2009.

In 2009, over 7.2 million people were under some form of correctional supervision including:

Probation - court-ordered period of correctional supervision in the community generally as an alternative to incarceration. In some cases probation can be a combined sentence of incarceration followed by a period of community supervision. These data include adults under the jurisdiction of probation agency, regardless of supervision status (i.e., active supervision, inactive supervision, financial conditions only, warrant status, absconder status, in a residential/other treatment program, or supervised out of jurisdiction).

Prison - confinement in a state or federal correctional facility to serve a sentence of more than 1 year, although in some jurisdictions the length of sentence which results in prison confinement is longer.

Jail - confinement in a local jail while pending trial,

awaiting sentencing, serving a sentence that is usually less than 1 year, or awaiting transfer to other facilities after conviction.

Parole - period of conditional supervised release in the community following a prison term, including prisoners released to parole either by a parole board decision (discretionary parole) or according to provisions of a statute (mandatory parole). These data include adults under the jurisdiction of a parole agency, regardless of supervision status (i.e., active supervision, inactive supervision, financial conditions only, absconder status, or supervised out of state).

Highlights include the following:

- The U.S. murder arrest rate in 2009 was about half of what it was in the early 1980s. Over the 30-year period ending in 2009, the adult arrest rate for murder fell **57%,** while the juvenile arrest rate fell **44%.**

- From 1980 to 2009, the black forcible rape arrest rate declined **70%,** while the white arrest rate fell **31%.**

- Between 1980 and 2009, while the adult arrest rate for drug possession or use grew **138%,** the juvenile arrest rate increased **33%.** Similarly, from 1980 to 2009, the increase in the arrest rate for drug sale or manufacture was greater for adults **(77%) than for juveniles (31%).**

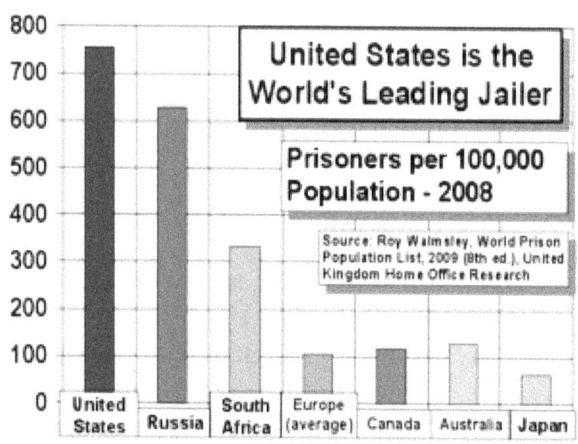

__The United States has the highest documented__

__incarceration rate in the world (743 per 100,000__

__population)__, Russia has the second highest rate (577 per

100,000), followed by Rwanda (561 per 100,000). As of

year-end 2009 the USA rate was 743 adults incarcerated in

prisons and jails per 100,000 population at year-end 2007 the

United States had less than 5% of the world's population and

23.4% of the world's prison and jail population (adult inmates).

By comparison the incarceration rate in <u>England</u> and <u>Wales</u> in February 2011 was 154 people imprisoned per 100,000 residents; the rate for <u>Norway</u> in May 2010 was 71 inmates per 100,000 <u>Netherlands</u> in April 2010 was 94 per 100,000 <u>Australia</u> in June 2010 was 133 per 100,000 and <u>New</u> <u>Zealand</u> in October 2010 was 203 per 100,000

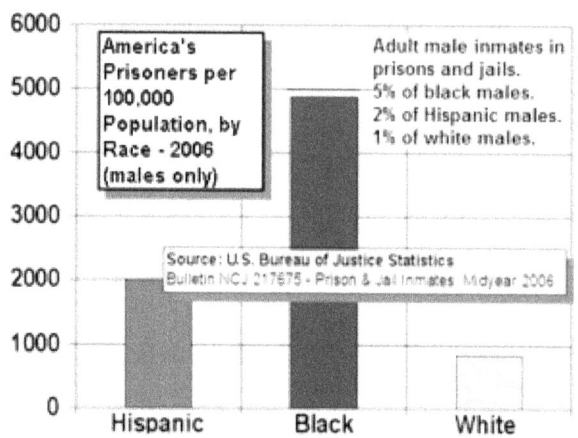

On June 30, **2006**, an estimated 4.8% of black non-Hispanic

men were in prison or jail, compared to 1.9% of Hispanic

men of any race and 0.7% of white non-Hispanic men. U.S.

Bureau of Justice Statistics.

4,800 per 100,000 Black males

1,900 per 100,000 Hispanic males

700 per 100,000 White males

This is reality!

Chapter I
The Black Holocaust

The United States of America (U.S.A.) is GUILTY of committing crimes against humanity. The first colonists brought slaves to Jamestown Virginia in 1619 to exploit and dehumanize them in ways unacceptable to mankind and God. These slaves who were captured like wild animals and herded into tightly clad transport ships had broken no laws, neither were they sold by other Africans, these slaves were unjustly taken against their will. White historians often quote other slaves and descendants of slaves as saying that "slaves captured and sold other slaves for rum and spices". While, I doubt very seriously that this ever happened, we must reflect back a little farther and ask ourselves how did the Africans know that they would be given rum and spices for captured slaves? Was there a bargain in place and if so who initiated the deal?

Please let me state clearly that this is not a white folk bashing book. This is a reality book! It never surprises me that every time my books are released, I get calls from many people who feel that I am bashing white folks/European Americans. Please let me list my disclaimer right here. I love white folks just like I love black folks, however, I have been hand-picked by my God to spent the rest of my life sitting on the wall as a watchman in America and speaking up for my people. Some folks may find the contents of this book hard to swallow and that is okay. When I write a book, I do not write based on whether or not people will like its contents or not, I write all of my books based on what I perceive to be the truth! And I've come to believe and know that the truth will make all of us free and if God be for you and the whole world be against you still ain't nobody against you.

Black folks in America were exploited on the way to Jamestown Virginia in 1619, they have been exploited in every place their feet have trod and they are still catching hell in America today. African Americans have bared the burdens of white folks for almost four hundred years in the U.S.A. and continue to do so even unto this day. Just because the law has changed which said that black folks were no longer considered to be 3/5 of a human the practice of enslaving and exploiting the labor of blacks continue to abound in the United States. The first settlers in the U.S.

worked African Americans like beast without compensating them. Black folks were counted as three-fifth human and degraded to the status of chattel. Additionally, their labor, families, wives and the knowledge of who they were as a people were all exploited. Black folks were not only considered chattel (a lower species of human and a grade slightly higher than an animal) but they were also treated like animals such as mules and donkeys.

African Americans who were forced to make the trip through the middle passage were stuffed into the hull of ships, chained like dogs, forced to lie in vomit, blood and feces. The women were chained naked in many cases, sexually exploited and assaulted in open view and no one pleaded their cause because they were viewed as animals (sub-human). Historians have written how the sharks followed the ships waiting for dead bodies to be casted overboard. Slavery and the slave trade was the greatest act of injustice the world has ever known period! No other race of people, the Jews, Japanese, native Americans etc. have suffer the violence, killings, maiming, psychological conditioning, exploitations, and degradations as African Americans. No other nation of people have suffered nearly as long as the African Americans and yet in the words of the great poet Maya Angelou "Still We Rise" just like the Phoenix we to rise from the ashes; African Americans in 2012 continue to rise. Once again, I make the injection here "If God be for you and the world be against you still aint nobody against you". Slavery was and still is the greatest crime ever committed by humanity against humanity that the world has ever known and will ever know. Black folks have endured hundreds of years of suffering, being kidnapped, maimed, robbed, dehumanized, broken, exploited and yet our spirits have not been broken and still we rise. Blacks who survived the middle passage arrived in America to find themselves being auctioned like animals, separated from their families and unable to communicate in their native dialect. These slaves were transported to plantations where they worked from sun up to sun down in the cotton fields and made cotton "King" throughout the southern parts of the United States.

Slaves made their white slave masters filthy rich yet they received no compensation. Today in America there are several lawyers and grassroots organizations advocating that the descendants of slaves be compensated for all of the toils of their early descendants yet no significant progress has been made. When Dr. King spoke on that famous day in August of 1963 he stated that America had written a check and the check came back marked insufficient funds yet he refused to believe that the vault of justice was bankrupt. Today (2012) America has written another check to African Americans and the money is in the bank, but in my opinion the check has been stamped "Stop Payment". It is stamped as such because there are many arrogant Americans who feel that black folks are only looking for a handout and that they do not deserve reparations or any compensation for the free labor of their parents, grandparents and great-grandparents. How ludicrous, if the law is to protect and compensate for misdeeds, broken contracts, labor violations then why aren't African Americans being compensated? Many states and their governments have made public apologies for how they treated our great grandmothers and great great-grandfathers but not one of them have put tried to make it right. If white folks in America could pay the Japanese for keeping them in lockdown for three years during World War II, they ought to be able to pay the descendants of slaves for keeping them in lockdown for three hundred years. Until there is justice for the millions of African American slaves whose blood continues to cry from the ground in America, there will NEVER be any peace! Black folks will not accept white America just treating us any kind of way and not having the decency to say I am sorry and putting their words into action.

21

If it had not been for free slave labor many white folks would not be in the position that they are in and if black folks were able to reap the profits that they made for their slave masters, many black folks would not be in the shape that they are in.

Finally in 1863, Abraham Lincoln signed the emancipation proclamation that freed the slaves from the plantations, but this proclamation did not free them from servitude. Many slaves took advantage of their new found freedom and traveled to the north where they thought they could be free indeed! However, there were many slaves in the south who for many reasons more than I could number decided to stay in the south and work as sharecroppers. These slaves were freed overnight and told that they were free to leave! Where do you go with nothing? They were promised forty acres and a mule, but black folks are still waiting for the forty acres and the mule today. Almost one hundred and fifty years later and black folks are still waiting for the forty acres and a mule. I doubt that I will see this payback anytime in my lifetime. The Emancipation Proclamation did not bring an end to black folk's problems; in fact it heightened the tensions among blacks and whites and led to the creation of the infamous group known as the Klu Klux Klan.

The Klu Klux Klan was one of the first terrorist organizations in the United States. Osama Bin Laden's Al quada Network did not have nor has anything on these Southern cowards who rode around on horses with sheets over their heads terrorizing black folks in the south. The Klan felt that it was their responsibility to keep black folks in their places and they did so by any means necessary, including hanging, tar and feathering, drowning and using any lynching methods necessary to strike fear in the hearts of black folks. Today the Klan has traded in their sheets for suits, robes and uniforms. The 21st century Klan can be seen on Sunday morning delivering a sermon from the pulpit fully clad with his cross and bible preaching separation of the races. He can be seen on Monday morning at the District Courthouse some of them have police uniforms on, some serve as District Attorneys and some even have their black robes on but exact white justice on the thousands of minorities that appear before them each year. The Klan is everywhere!

Prior to 1863, black folks were not subject to incarceration as a general rule because they were considered personal property (chattel) of the plantation owners. You didn't put cows and pigs in prison so in their twisted philosophy slaves fell under the same category.

Once slaves were freed, white folks began to lose money; they no longer had slaves to plant and harvest their cotton crops so they used politics and legislation to return ex-slaves back to the plantation.

In the early 1870's vagrancy laws began to appear with new meanings. Everyone that the legal authorities (police, sheriffs, courts etc.) came into contact with had to have a permanent residence and proof that they had paid their one dollar poll tax or they were placed in jail for three to five years. This was the beginning of the legal enactment and enforcement of laws aimed specifically at black folks. These undocumented laws gave birth to the Black Codes (laws that were enforced but were not pass through legislation) and Jim Crow Laws (laws aimed at black folks to keep them powerless) of the south. These ex-slaves had just been freed, so they had no homestead, further they were sharecroppers so they were paid in food and one pair of overalls or one dress per year so they had no cash to pay poll taxes and as a result they were placed in jails and prisons. These underhanded acts were responsible for birthing the infamous convict lease system, which W.E. Dubois wrote about at the end of the nineteenth century. The convict lease system was a scheme devised by the white man to place freed slaves back on the plantation. Once ex-slaves were arrested for not having a permanent residence or for not paying their poll taxes, they were warehoused in jails and auctioned to private companies (plantation owners, railroad executives, canal diggers, etc) and other forms of employment white folks were not willing to do or could not do. These companies leased these black prisoners and put them to work digging canals through the swamps, subjecting them to malaria. These prisoners were also performing backbreaking work laying railroad tracks, and of course harvesting cotton and other crops for wealthy plantation owners. These companies in turn paid the state monies for the inmate's labor. In this regard the governor of each of the states that participated in the convict labor system became the quote-unquote new plantation boss.

Now the white folks in the south had succeeded once again in getting black folks right back on the plantation despite the Emancipation Proclamation. The states, plantation owners, and private companies were all getting paid and once again exploiting the ex-slaves as before.

As the twentieth century approached, the industrial era began to emerge in the United States and factories and machinery began to mass produce goods and machine muscle began to replace human muscle. John Dewey's cotton gin began to be used on the plantation, caterpillar machinery began to be used to excavate rivers and canals and companies were able to mass produce goods on the assembly line. The need for convict labor began to dwindle as states began to enjoy blighted eras of prosperity thanks to the newfound machinery and the orders for more goods from other countries.

As the needs and demands for black muscle decreased, blacks began to migrate to the north where they found a new world. In the north blacks were not only free, but they were business owners. Blacks experienced a new era called the black renaissance in which they excelled in the arts, sciences, entrepreneurship and the likes. Blacks for the first time began to enjoy, appreciate and value their independence. While blacks in the north were enjoying their new found freedom, blacks in the south were being faced with a new phenomenon which equated to a threat of equality.

White folks in the south have always indicated that blacks only made up 13-25% of any states population since the first black folks arrived in 1619. If black folks only made up a small percentage of these states' population, then why would the Klu Klux Klan brutally attack black folks who were simply trying to vote, if their percentages indicated that they could not win anyway? I have never believed that black folks only made up 12.7% of the U.S. population. We must be critical thinkers! For 300 plus years black folks were bred like animals to keep stock up on the plantations, while white folks have continued to have between one to three children in their households. I have been and still am leery of the U.S.

Census. I am a conspiracy theorist in this respect because, I know that a census is only as accurate as the person (s) conducting it. Black folks do not fill out census for the most part and if censuses are the only mechanisms used to determine population, we are seriously undercounted. Black folks have warrants on them, they are wanted for child support, traffic tickets, and as a general fact black folks just don't like to sit down and write, especially if there are no immediate incentives for them. If the U.S. Government really wants to get an accurate census of black folks in America all they need to do is grant them criminal and civil immunity and pay 100 to each person and 300 dollars to each family completing the census, our percentage in the population would probably triple. It is my contentions that

31

the census is a political tool used by white folks to create a sense of hopelessness for black folks. If black folks only make up 13% of the population why are so many barriers being put up to stop black folks from voting like felon disenfranchisement?

Slavery and Incarceration has been served the greatest crimes against humanity. We will never forget! Black Folks will never forget slavery or the mass incarceration of black folks in America because we know that both of these acts were intentional and are perpetrated by powerbrokers greedy for ill-gotten gain. This black holocaust has been going on for 400 years and is still growing!

Chapter II

The Real Reason Behind Black Imprisonment in the United States

Why are so many black folks in jail in America? Simply put, black folks are in jail in America for several reasons, I will list them in an order based on importance.

First and foremost, blacks are exploited and placed in jails and prisons because incarceration is a means used by white folks to have jobs and maintain job security which in turn pays for their mortgages, car notes, living expenses and food etc. This is the most important reason that black folks are in jail.

I have had and still have serious reservations as to why so many black folks are incarcerated in the United States. Every since blacks folks were semi-freed from slavery they have been targeted by white folks who have made it no secret to keep them in servitude. In America today jails and prisons are filled to capacity with inmates whose only crime is that they are poor! Malcolm X stated that what white folks were seeing in him was the hate that their hate toward him produced. Mass prison incarceration is a result of white folks needing money to pay their enormous mortgages, car notes, insurances, college tuition, and their general living expenses. Make no mistake about it; white folks have put paying their living expenses as the number one priority even if it means locking up every Negro in the community. As Darnell

Hawkins, has alluded to in his book, black life is not valued as much as white life in America. Black folks are still looked upon as being second-class citizens and although theorists have disqualified Lombroso's theory that criminals were akin to primates and throw-backs in civilization, the African American in the U.S. is still treated as he is some sub-human species. I personally get tired of waking up in the morning looking at the news and seeing black faces in handcuffs, police cars, lying under coroner sheets surrounded by yellow police tape, on surveillance video cameras etc.

In the state of Louisiana, you can find many small private satellite prisons. These prisons are a direct result of white politicians cashing in on the Negro prisoner cash crop. When industries and enterprise leave small rural communities in

Louisiana, their local state representatives or senators go down to Baton Rouge and plead for a local prison to jump start their economy. Private jails have become the new stimulus plans for rural America.

Small private prisons supply the community with approximately 300 jobs and make the economy robust again for these white folks. Everybody in the community get in on the action and the majority of their clientele are poor black folks who are separated from their children, parents, friends etc. Do these white folks care about this, no! If these folks being locked up and punished were killers, rapists, aggravated assaulters, child molesters or any violent offenders that were causing a threat to the community, I would not open my mouth because they would be in need of incarceration, but 75% of the prisoners that I am alluding to here are non-violent offenders whose crimes are selling drugs or possession of drugs. Let's not get this twisted! When white folks say that they have removed a drug dealer off the street we think about folks with large operations but in reality if you have three rocks worth $30.00 in a plastic bag, you are charged with possession with intent to distribute. This individual is facing 30 years in prison for $30.00 worth of dope. That is ridiculous! If this person is sentenced to 10 years in prison, we as taxpayers will pay an average of $30,000 dollars a year to keep this person incarcerated. Over a ten year period we will spend 300,000.00 to keep this person incarcerated. This 300,000.00 will pay off car notes, mortgage notes, send several children to colleges, and provide car insurance etc for the exploiters.

This is wrong! This is a serious crime against humanity!

Sigmund Freud said that sex was the dominant impulse! I

say that for those that exploit the millions of African

Americans in the U.S. money is the dominant impulse.

When these private prisons open in small rural communities,

doctors, restaurants, carpenters, electricians, bankers,

utilities, baby-sitters, gas-stations and every business in town

profit including the politician who closed the deal! This is

cruel but it is a reality. No one gives a hoot about the poor

black prisoner! He is treated like an animal, a primate, a sub-

human and then those in charge of his custody have the

audacity to say we treat these Negroes better than they were

being treated in the streets as to say that they are better off there. How ludicrous! The bottom line of this is that if white folks were not reaping windfalls from exploiting these prisoners, the prisons would be empty. Prisons are not trying to rehabilitate prisoners they are merely warehousing black folks all over the country!

Poverty is the second leading cause to black imprisonment. When folks are broke and cannot provide for themselves many of them result to crime, drugs, thievery and innovative means to live.

It does not take a rocket scientist to figure out that people who don't have money make choices much different from people who do have money. Poverty is the 2nd leading cause of crime in theory but ranks number one in practical application. Let's face it; the majority of black folks in

America have incomes that are well below the median income for Americans. African-Americans have the largest percentage of poverty in the United States. When it comes to income, black folks and Native Americans fall way below the norm. As a result of this poverty many black folks have resorted to getting money by any means necessary. While I do not condone crime in any respect, I must truly say that I understand crime and I understand why some people will result to criminal activity. It is very easy for some folks who are making fifty, sixty, one hundred thousand dollars to say that no matter how hard things get, or how poor people are they should not steal, rob or burglarize! That is easy to say when you have everything that you need and your refrigerator is full of steaks and fillet mignon, but when your utilities are due, mortgage is due, children are hungry, many folks have to make ends meets by any means necessary.

In criminal justice there is a theory called the rational choice theory that purports that people make rational choices before committing a crime, in this respect, I believe they do. When you have tried to get a job and no one is hiring, everywhere you go employers are telling you they will call, but no one is calling and your bills are getting further behind! It is at times like these that black folks and white folks begin to stress and they find themselves drinking more, smoking more, acting out more as a matter of escape and their behaviors lead to low self-esteem and hopelessness and eventually survival by any means necessary. When a person is in this state, they are susceptible to doing almost anything! Anything that sounds good and is capable of putting money in the pocket with what seems to be minimal risk is a good idea. Many black folks are in prison today because they made irrational choices when they were stressing for money. Money is the great equalizer! Poverty only serves to put black folks further and further behind. Poverty is the MOTHER of CRIME! White folks will quickly say that black folks have the same opportunities as they have. That is not true! Many white folks have old money in their families. Black folks did not receive their 40 acres or their mule. African Americans have been exploited from the beginning and we are still catching hell in America. Until the playing fields are equal and black folks are truly given the same opportunities to work as white folks, crime will remain constant. Poverty is the mother of crime (Andrus, Tracy 2012)!

The lack of formal education is the third leading cause of incarceration for African Americans. Approximately sixty-five percent of prisoners in the U.S. do not have a high school education. Education is a major factor and plays a major role in the prison schema. Students who do not complete high school are much more likely to enter prison in the U.S. African American youth have the highest dropout rate in the U.S. these children are much more likely to enter prison for a number of reasons. Not having a high school education usually means making less money, working on jobs with little or no benefits and being unable to purchase a nice home or car which is the American dream. All of this

43

leads to a person's vulnerability to become an innovator or choose illegitimate means to earn money. People in this cycle turn to drugs, gambling, fencing and other illegal means to supplement their incomes, thereby putting themselves at a greater risk for arrest, conviction and imprisonment.

We must do a better job of educating our children, especially black boys. Black folks catch enough hell getting a job with a high school diploma. Those without a high school diploma compound their problems by not having a high school diploma. There is very little that a person can do in the U.S. without a high school diploma besides wash dishes, mop floors, empty garbage and work on menial jobs. It is a known fact that the higher the degree of education a person attains the higher their wages will be. It is therefore imperative that we provide schools and alternative schools to meet the needs of our children. They must be educated by any means necessary! If we fail to educate them, we are really setting them up for a life of poverty, crime and stress. The denial and unavailability of legitimate jobs are the fourth leading cause of African American imprisonment.

It cannot be overemphasized how important it is to have jobs available for our youth and our adults. Children, who grow up with a good work ethic, usually retain a good work ethic throughout life. When I was a child, there was a program called the CETA program which provided jobs for high school students between the ages of 15 and 19 years old. These programs helped to instill a great work ethic in those

45

who took advantage of these programs. Once a person works and enjoys working and receiving a decent wage there is something about that person that is never the same again. People who work on jobs that pay a decent wage are much less likely to engage in criminal behavior. People who work on jobs that pay a decent wage and provide decent benefits are much more accountable and have higher self-esteem. It feels good to be able to provide one's family with a nice home, car, insurance and a decent form of living. People who make a decent living and are able to pay their bills are much less likely to engage in any criminal conduct. When people make money and have money in their pockets they are much less likely to rob and steal! We don't see people like Bill Gates and Donald Trump breaking in buildings or holding up

7-elevens because these people have money. The people that we see committing acts such as these are those who are broke.

Many of my white and several of my black brothers and sisters have said that many black folks do not want to work; they are lazy and want something for nothing! First of all black folks cannot be too lazy, they built America and made America what it is today! Many African Americans refuse to work for the meager wages that employers want to pay. There is a consensus among many black folks that says that black folks have worked for nothing long enough in America. I often tell folks that black folks do not want something for nothing, they want something for something. We are now living in a global society and the world is flat for some and this means that employees know exactly what CEOs are making and this information has a direct impact on worker morale. The bottom line here is that black folks need good meaningful jobs. Neither black nor white folks can support their families on minimum wages. Why should a person work for $7.15 per hour when they can make 500.00 a day being a street pharmacist? Some people are willing to take the chance because they view the profits derived as being worth the risk.

Racism, prejudice and discriminatory laws are the fifth leading cause of imprisonment for African Americans. The fifth leading cause of incarceration for African Americans is racism, prejudice and discrimination. Most white folks in

America have always exhibited racism! It is because of racist laws that many black folks are locked up in prison.

The heat of compassion is the sixth leading cause of incarceration for African Americans.

Heat of passion is the only cause of crime by black folks that cannot be related to whites or income.

The seventh leading cause is economic and political power-threat. Most criminologist and persons who are trained in criminal justice know that these are the seven primary causes for mass African American incarceration in the United States. According to Hubert Blalock (1967), when minority populations threaten the economic, political or financial power of majority populations, they will resort to any means necessary to retain their power.

49

As we have entered into the 21st century in the year of our Lord 2012, I do not see any relief in sight for African Americans as it relates to prison incarceration from the Caucasian race. If African Americans are to save their sons and daughters from the beast in the bottomless pit (aka lockdown) then we as a people will have to pull up our own bootstraps and help to create jobs, educational opportunities, position ourselves to get into higher political positions, higher law enforcement position and become producers and not just consumers. The prison industrial complex in America is exploiting black folks at alarming rates. Black folks are being warehoused in jails and prisons for extended periods of time for what was once considered petty-misdemeanor crimes. As the need for money has risen among municipalities, so has the need for more prisoners. Black have served as the scapegoat for white folks for a long time as illustrated in chapter one, but now the time has come to break free of the chains that have squeezed us so tight and prevented us from achieving, prospering and determining our own destiny.

Black folks are also incarcerated to keep their power diluted at the voting polls and reduce the black population.

Hubert Blalock wrote about power-threat in 1967. In his hypothesis he suggested that anytime black folks or any minority approach a level in the population where they are able to threaten the economic and/or political dominance of the majority population that the majority population will result to any means necessary to maintain economic or political power. These actions may include mass murder, genocide, distributing drugs in the neighborhoods, mass incarceration, unemployment and under-employment etc. Ida B. Wells also wrote and spoke about the lynching of African Americans in the U.S. Many of these lynchings were the result of African Americans entrepreneurs competing against white entrepreneurs. The story of Oklahoma's thriving black community being burned down was another example of whites not wanting to face competition from blacks.

Chapter III

Who Is To Be Blamed For The Black Disproportionate Incarceration Rates In The United States?

Who is really to be blamed for the astronomical incarceration rates in the black community? There is no doubt that we as African Americans cannot put all of the blame on white folks for our high incarceration rates. I understand that black folks do not want to work for meager wages and that we have never really received adequate pay for the work that we have performed, however, we are responsible for the decisions that we make.

White folks can be blamed for excessive African American incarceration for several reasons, including the fact that white folks created hopeless communities by not giving black folks the equivalent of 40 acres and a mule to start with. White folks also monopolized industries and the economy in such a way that it is hard, very hard for African Americans to pull themselves up by the bootstraps. In America, the only way that one can compete is if they have money. Capitalism is built on having capital! If you don't have capital you will almost never succeed in a capitalist society. White folks make millions of dollars by trading stocks, yet very few black folks know the first thing about the stock markets.

To what extent do we hold black folks accountable for committing crimes and having such high imprisonment and jail rates? Black folks should be held accountable for the bad decisions that we make, but only if we make the bad decisions after we have had access to legitimate employment. I believe that in the social contract the greater good for the majority should also include decent and stable jobs. In essence, I am saying that we cannot blame black folks, white folks or any other folks for committing crimes unless we have provided those persons with an opportunity to have meaningful employment.

Politicians are on the list. Politicians play a very big role in the continuation of black mass incarceration. Politicians always inflame the consciousness of constituents in relations to crime and use crime as one of their agenda items even in cities, states and counties that do not have serious crime problems. Politicians will always use crime as a part of their platforms. Many politicians are guilty of passing laws that they know will adversely affect black folks, such as crack cocaine laws, drug conviction laws, and felony disenfranchisement laws. Many of the laws passed by the House and the senate are really unnecessary; because these newly enacted laws only embellish laws that are already in effect.

The media is also responsible for portraying negative pictures, images and propaganda that make black folks akin to beast and dangerous predators. In many cases the media will show the faces and arrest of black folks on the news, but will not show the faces of white folks who are guilty of committing similar crimes. The media has the power to persuade people to think in manners that maybe inconsistent and unwarranted based on the facts. Not all black folks are criminals, yet the media in many cases stereotype black folks in a manner that makes all black folk look like they are thugs, murders, dope dealers, thieves and just don't give a dam!

The economy also plays a major role in determining whether or not black folks will be incarcerated. As long as the economy is good and white and black folks are making a decent wage, crime will be down and so will incarceration. The economy is the pulse of the nation. When everyone's house notes, car notes, insurance and other bills are paid and they have extra money to enjoy, crime will diminish. On the other hand, when the economy is dull, work is scarce, unemployment and underemployment is high, crime and imprisonment will also be high. When white folks can no longer pay their bills they increase the arrest and execution of warrants for minorities. The increased arrest rates and warehousing of these prisons account for an increase in revenue and salaries for white folks who in turn pay their bills through incarceration and exploitation of the masses of poor folks. What a shame and a disgrace to humanity!

Economic and political power threats are also major factors that determine whether or not black folks will be incarcerated. When white folks perceive that their political or economic power is being threatened they will result to any means to stay in power. When minorities begin to gain equal footing and trade among one another, great things happen.

Population control (eugenics) –incarceration serves to diminish the black race by great numbers. Approximately 1.5 million less babies are born each year as a result of black folks being incarcerated.

The black church has not done her part in helping to curb the incarceration rates of African Americans. The black church could do so much for the black race, yet most preachers and pastors are more concerned about building the largest church in the area. The black church must actively participate in gaining meaningful employment for its constituents. I personally would like to take my hat off to those churches that have tried and are still trying to empower their communities through efforts of providing early childhood learning centers, great community services, medical services, community development, providing adequate medical services, etc.

Chapter IV

Capitalization, Prisonization and the Just Another Black Man Locked Up Attitude Among Criminal Justice Practitioners and Politicians

To say that many politicians do not care about the poor would really be an understatement. Politicians always make "getting tough on crime" a high priority. Why? I have yet to hear many politician say, I am going to get tough on unemployment, tough on creating jobs for the poor, tough on dismantling the projects and the project mentality which seems to breed more illiteracy, welfare, babies without daddies, more delinquency and definitely more crime. It is time for black folks, white folks, red folks and yellow folks to start asking our politicians what exactly are they going to do if we elect them and if you don't like the answer and you do not think it is fair, groom your own candidate. The ballot box is the most powerful tool in the world and when you mix your vote with your hope and connect it to your passion for your God we all win in the end, because now we become more concerned with what is right and not necessarily what is popular. There were many older whites who did not vote for President Obama not because he was not speaking their language but simple because he was black and that was not popular in their homes, churches and on their jobs. Let's face it some white folks will not vote for a black man period, I don't care if he is the only one in the race and sadly we have some black folks who will not vote for white folks under any

61

circumstances period. Racism is alive and well in the United States and can be seen in our everyday business transactions, the way we live, on our jobs, in politics and even in the churches that we attend!

The criminal Justice system in America is the biggest farce ever created by man. There is a saying in the African American community that" if something does not start right it will not end up right". If that is the case our prison system will never be right, never! The prison system in America was designed to keep freed black folks on the plantation and provide free labor to business owners in the south after reconstruction and the signing of the Emancipation Proclamation. The prison system in America is a multi-billion dollar warehousing enterprise ran on the premise that it must continue its existence to keep the bad people off the streets. Let me be the first person to say that of course we need prisons and there are people who will in my opinion never learn from their mistakes unless they have a personal encounter with God himself. But, my overall opinion of the criminal justice system (police, courts and corrections) is that this is a money making operation that exploits people from all races but especially the poor.

Politicians who come from areas where the economy is bad seems to resort to introducing proposals to construct prison farms as a means to boost the economy. When businesses and other industries move out of rural areas in the south, the solution to all of the people's problems according to many politicians are to build private prisons to generate some revenue for these distressed areas. These politicians do not build prisons with the thought of maybe we will get some inmates, but they build prisons with the thoughts of filling them up. Empty prisons do not make money. The economy has gotten so bad to where inmates are now expanding prisons, building new prison facilities from the foundations to the roof-tops and, little do they know that these prisons are being built for their kids, grandkids and great grandkids. We must stop the madness of over incarcerating our people. We will never build our way out of crime, because crime is perception based on our beliefs. What's legal in California may not be legal in Texas. What is legal in the U.S. may not be legal in Amsterdam. Crime is what we say crime is and the punishments for acts are what w say the punishments are.

As long as black folks are disproportionately represented in law enforcement, politics and businesses and do not step up to the plate through its churches, businesses, civic organizations, and citizenry, we will continue to be treated like second class citizens. Crime does not run the criminal justice system, capitalization does and if the day ever comes in which prisons do not make gross profits you will quickly see the demise of what we now know as the prison system! There are many private investors who have great interest in the privatization of prisons. All of this is being done in the name of money. When prisons are built concrete suppliers, steel fabricators, kitchen equipment suppliers, painters, mattress producers, sheet companies etc all make money. Some folks are put to work but many children and spouses suffer and become dependent on the welfare system because the primary bread winner is taken out of the house. In America we say that the laws must be utilitarian which means that we should support greatest good for the greatest number of citizens. Are laws that take guardians away from children for petty drug offenses in the greatest interest of the child, economy, and institutions? Please!

Many politicians subscribe to the lock them up and throw away the key attitude for criminals because they believe that the majority these criminals are not their constituents. Most republican politicians do not feel that they owe anything to anyone who is not part of their constituency and they cannot count on your vote anyway. It's all about politics. It is therefore no problem for me to say that there are many politicians, individuals (black and white), who have the same mind set which says if they (black or white) commit a crime lock them up and throw away the key. These beliefs are much more aligned with conservatives who are usually republicans than they are with liberal democrats.

Chapter V

The Prison Industrial Complex: A Crime against Humanity

The prison industrial complex is the greatest scheme America has ever seen! What is the difference between the mindset of those in the 1890s and the year 2012s? Nothing! White folks are still locking up many black folks for extended periods of time for menial offenses. They are still working them for very little or no money on prison plantations. Black folks are continuing to build prisons for their children, grandchildren and their great-great grandchildren. What a shame! What is wrong with us as black people? Why do we just sit by and allow our relatives, children and friends to be punished unjustly without saying a thing? We are too passive when it comes to speaking up for what we know is right. Giving a man or woman ten years in prison for 3 pieces of rock cocaine worth 30.00 does not make any sense whatsoever, unless you are looking at crime from the crime pays ideology. Yes, crime pays many house notes, car notes, college tuitions, trips to Disneyland, etc for those entrusted with keeping us locked up. When will we learn that this prison system that we are witnessing in the U.S.A. is not designed to rehabilitate us, neither is it a system used to house those who pose a danger to American citizens. The American prison system is an elaborate multi-billion dollar enterprise fueled and funded by wealthy politicians, investors and business men. This enterprise assures the dominant white males that they will remain in power as long as they arrest, convict and imprison blacks and other minorities. Being convicted of a crime strips a man of his net worth immediately and in many cases perpetually. You never outlive the stigma attached to you once you have been convicted of a felony. Regardless to what job you hold, you still must answer the question in the affirmative every time it is asked.

Today, prisoners make just about everything that is needed to operate prisons and business enterprises for each state's government. Prisoners make furniture, computers, beds, mattresses, business cards, etc. They grow and raise 90% of the food they eat. They are self-contained. Before long, they will be building power plants if they are not doing so already. They build prisons and other facilities from the ground up. Some of the most advanced architects, bricklayers, electricians, plumbers, lawyers, mathematicians, preachers, laborers are in America's jails and prisons.

In prison you don't have a choice as to whether you will work or not, either you work or go to the hole (lockdown). If prison officials can find jobs for everyone in prison when they are working for nothing, why can't these same officials with the aid of the U.S. government find work with decent wages for all of these men and women when they are released? Are we being forced into prison because of the lack of jobs and the lack of suitable alternatives to earn a decent wage? It is time to start asking questions and demanding answers.

According to the Prison Policy Initiative:

Incarceration is not an equal opportunity punishment

On December 31, 2005, there were 2,193,798 people in U.S. prisons and jails. The United States incarcerates a greater share of its population, 737 per 100,000 residents, than any other country on the planet. But when you break down the statistics you see that incarceration is not an equal opportunity punishment.

U.S. incarceration rates by race, June 30, 2004:

71

- **Whites:** 393 per 100,000
- **Latinos:** 957 per 100,000
- **Blacks:** 2,531 per 100,000

Gender is an important "filter" in regards to who goes to prison or jail, June 30, 2005:

- **Females:** 129 per 100,000
- **Males:** 1,371 per 100,000

Look at just the males by race, and the incarceration rates become even more frightening, June 30, 2005:

- **White males:** 709 per 100,000
- **Latino males:** 1,856 per 100,000
- **Black males:** 4,682 per 100,000

If you look at males aged 25-29 and by race, you can see what is going on even clearer, June 30, 2005:

- **For White males ages 25-29:** 1,682 per 100,000.
- **For Latino males ages 25-29:** 3,884 per 100,000.
- **For Black males ages 25-29:** 11,955 per 100,000. (That's 11.9% of Black men in their late 20s.)

Or you can make some international comparisons:
South Africa under Apartheid was internationally
condemned as a racist society.

- **South Africa under apartheid (1993), Black males:** 851 per 100,000
- **U.S. under George Bush (2004), Black males:** 4,919 per 100,000

What does it mean that the leader of the "free world" locks

up its Black males at a rate 5.8 times higher than the most

openly racist country in the world?

US prisons have become big business, housing 25% of all

the people in the world behind bars, the largest prison

population on the planet. In a frenzy of criminal justice, we

have turned our backs on the founding principles of this

nation to produce state and federal prisons at an alarming

rate -- in the 1990s, opening 1 every 15 days in depressed

rural towns and communities. Private correctional companies are entering the industry, appearing on the NY stock exchange, with an eye on the bottom line. Under this prison-industrial complex, we are locking up 1 in 3 young black men in this nation, moving them far from home, and stripping them of the right to vote, the possibility of holding decent jobs and the dignity of supporting themselves and their families. US prisons are holding the strangest of reunions: grandfathers, fathers and sons behind bars. There is no paying of their debt to society, no clean slate..... HUMAN rights organizations, as well as political and social ones, are condemning what they are calling a new form of inhumane exploitation in the United States, where they say a prison population of up to 2 million – mostly Black and

Hispanic – are working for various industries for a pittance. For the tycoons who have invested in the prison industry, it has been like finding a pot of gold. They don't have to worry about strikes or paying unemployment insurance, vacations or comp time. All of their workers are full-time, and never arrive late or are absent because of family problems; moreover, if they don't like the pay of 25 cents an hour and refuse to work, they are locked up in isolation cells.

There are approximately 2 million inmates in state, federal and private prisons throughout the country. According to California Prison Focus, "no other society in human history has imprisoned so many of its own citizens." The figures show that the United States has locked up more people than any other country: a half million more than China, which has a population five times greater than the U.S. Statistics reveal that the United States holds 25% of the world's prison population, but only 5% of the world's people. From less than 300,000 inmates in 1972, the jail population grew to 2 million by the year 2000. In 1990 it was one million. Ten years ago there were only five private prisons in the country, with a population of 2,000 inmates; now, there are 100, with 62,000 inmates. It is expected that by the coming decade, the number will hit 360,000, according to reports. What has happened over the last 10 years? Why are there so many prisoners?

"The private contracting of prisoners for work fosters incentives to lock people up. Prisons depend on this income. Corporate stockholders who make money off prisoners' work lobby for longer sentences, in order to expand their workforce. The system feeds itself," says a study by the Progressive Labor Party, which accuses the prison industry of being "an imitation of Nazi Germany with respect to forced slave labor and concentration camps."

The prison industry complex is one of the fastest-growing industries in the United States and its investors are on Wall Street. "This multimillion-dollar industry has its own trade exhibitions, conventions, websites, and mail-order/Internet catalogs. It also has direct advertising campaigns, architecture companies, construction companies, investment

houses on Wall Street, plumbing supply companies, food

supply companies, armed security, and padded cells in a

large variety of colors."

According to the Left Business Observer, the federal prison

industry produces 100% of all military helmets, ammunition

belts, bullet-proof vests, ID tags, shirts, pants, tents, bags,

and canteens. Along with war supplies, prison workers

supply 98% of the entire market for equipment assembly

services; 93% of paints and paintbrushes; 92% of stove

assembly; 46% of body armor; 36% of home appliances;

30% of headphones/microphones/speakers; and 21% of

office furniture. Airplane parts, medical supplies, and much more: prisoners are even raising seeing-eye dogs for blind people.

CRIME GOES DOWN, JAIL POPULATION GOES UP

According to reports by human rights organizations, these are the factors that increase the profit potential for those who invest in the prison industry complex:

• Jailing persons convicted of non-violent crimes, and long prison sentences for possession of microscopic quantities of illegal drugs. Federal law stipulates five years' imprisonment without possibility of parole for possession of 5 grams of crack or 3.5 ounces of heroin, and 10 years for possession of less than 2 ounces of rock-cocaine or crack. A sentence of 5 years for cocaine powder requires possession of 500 grams – 100 times more than the quantity of rock cocaine for the same sentence. Most of those who use cocaine powder are white, middle-class or rich people, while mostly Blacks and Latinos use rock cocaine. In Texas, a person may be sentenced for up to two years' imprisonment for possessing 4 ounces of marijuana. Here in New York, the 1973 Nelson Rockefeller anti-drug law provides for a mandatory prison sentence of 15 years to life for possession of 4 ounces of any illegal drug.

• The passage in 13 states of the "three strikes" laws (life in prison after being convicted of three felonies), made it necessary to build 20 new federal prisons. One of the most disturbing cases resulting from this measure was that of a prisoner who for stealing a car and two bicycles received three 25-year sentences.

HISTORY OF PRISON LABOR IN THE UNITED STATES

Prison labor has its roots in slavery. After the 1861-1865 Civil War, a system of "hiring out prisoners" was introduced in order to continue the slavery tradition. Freed slaves were charged with not carrying out their sharecropping commitments (cultivating someone else's land in exchange for part of the harvest) or petty thievery – which were almost never proven – and were then "hired out" for cotton picking, working in mines and building railroads. From 1870 until 1910 in the state of Georgia, 88% of hired-out convicts were

81

Black. In Alabama, 93% of "hired-out" miners were Black. In Mississippi, a huge prison farm similar to the old slave plantations replaced the system of hiring out convicts. The notorious Parchman plantation existed until 1972.

During the post-Civil War period, Jim Crow racial segregation laws were imposed on every state, with legal segregation in schools, housing, marriages and many other aspects of daily life. "Today, a new set of markedly racist laws is imposing slave labor and sweatshops on the criminal justice system, now known as the prison industry complex," comments the Left Business Observer.

Who is investing? At least 37 states have legalized the contracting of prison labor by private corporations that mount their operations inside state prisons. The list of such companies contains the cream of U.S. corporate society: IBM, Boeing, Motorola, Microsoft, AT&T, Wireless, Texas Instrument, Dell, Compaq, Honeywell, Hewlett-Packard, Nortel, Lucent Technologies, 3Com, Intel, Northern Telecom, TWA, Nordstrom's, Revlon, Macy's, Pierre Cardin, Target Stores, and many more. All of these businesses are excited about the economic boom generation by prison labor. Just between 1980 and 1994, profits went up from $392 million to $1.31 billion. Inmates in state penitentiaries generally receive the minimum wage for their work, but not all; in Colorado, they get about $2 per hour, well under the minimum. And in privately-run prisons, they receive as little as 17 cents per hour for a maximum of six hours a day, the equivalent of $20 per month. The highest-paying private prison is CCA in Tennessee, where prisoners receive 50 cents per hour for what they call "highly skilled positions." At those rates, it is no surprise that inmates find the pay in federal prisons to be very generous. There, they can earn $1.25 an hour and work eight hours a day, and sometimes overtime. They can send home $200-$300 per month.

Thanks to prison labor, the United States is once again an attractive location for investment in work that was designed for Third World labor markets. A company that operated a *maquiladora* (assembly plant in Mexico near the border) closed down its operations there and relocated to San

Quentin State Prison in California. In Texas, a factory fired its 150 workers and contracted the services of prisoner-workers from the private Lockhart Texas prison, where circuit boards are assembled for companies like IBM and Compaq.

Oregon State Representative Kevin Mannix recently urged Nike to cut its production in Indonesia and bring it to his state, telling the shoe manufacturer that "there won't be any transportation costs; we're offering you competitive prison labor (here)."

PRIVATE PRISONS

The prison privatization boom began in the 1980s, under the governments of Ronald Reagan and Bush Sr., but reached its height in 1990 under William Clinton, when Wall Street stocks were selling like hotcakes. Clinton's program for cutting the federal workforce resulted in the Justice Departments contracting of private prison corporations for the incarceration of undocumented workers and high-security inmates.

Private prisons are the biggest business in the prison industry complex. About 18 corporations guard 10,000 prisoners in 27 states. The two largest are Correctional Corporation of America (CCA) and Wackenhut, which together control 75%. Private prisons receive a guaranteed amount of money for each prisoner, independent of what it costs to maintain each one. According to Russell Boraas, a private prison administrator in Virginia, "the secret to low operating costs is having a minimal number of guards for the maximum number of prisoners." The CCA has an ultra-modern prison in Lawrenceville, Virginia, where five guards on dayshift and two at night watch over 750 prisoners. In these prisons, inmates may get their sentences reduced for "good behavior," but for any infraction, they get 30 days added – which means more profits for CCA. According to a study of New Mexico prisons, it was found that CCA inmates lost "good behavior time" at a rate eight times higher than those in state prisons.

IMPORTING AND EXPORTING INMATES

Profits are so good that now there is a new business: importing inmates with long sentences, meaning the worst criminals. When a federal judge ruled that overcrowding in Texas prisons was cruel and unusual punishment, the CCA signed contracts with sheriffs in poor counties to build and run new jails and share the profits. According to a December 1998 **Atlantic Monthly** magazine article, this program was backed by investors from Merrill-Lynch, Shearson-Lehman, American Express and Allstate, and the operation was scattered all over rural Texas. That state's governor, Ann Richards, followed the example of Mario Cuomo in New York and built so many state prisons that the market became flooded, cutting into private prison profits.

After a law signed by Clinton in 1996 – ending court supervision and decisions – caused overcrowding and violent, unsafe conditions in federal prisons, private prison corporations in Texas began to contact other states whose prisons were overcrowded, offering "rent-a-cell" services in the CCA prisons located in small towns in Texas. The commission for a rent-a-cell salesman is $2.50 to $5.50 per day per bed. The county gets $1.50 for each prisoner.

STATISTICS

Ninety-seven percent of 125,000 federal inmates have been convicted of non-violent crimes. It is believed that more than half of the 623,000 inmates in municipal or county jails are innocent of the crimes they are accused of. Of these, the majority are awaiting trial. Two-thirds of the one million state prisoners have committed non-violent offenses. Sixteen percent of the country's 2 million prisoners suffer from mental illness.

Chapter VI

The Collateral Effects of Disproportionate Black Incarceration in the U. S.

The more I travel throughout the United States, the more I realize that a vote less people is a hopeless people. I know and believe in my heart that God is the great almighty, but I also know that the greatest power available to man on earth aside from God comes through the ballot box. Why do you think that politicians make such a big deal out of disenfranchising criminals? There are many industrialized countries that do not disenfranchise their citizens for the commission of crimes. When the word criminal is spoken many folks including black folks envision a black man with a bandana, pants sagging etc. The words crime and criminal automatically evokes fear, anger and grave concern for many Americans but especially white Americans. White folks have almost always viewed themselves as the victims of crimes and black folks as the perpetrators. This is the reason that most white politicians will run on a platform in which getting tough on crime is their main theme. Getting tough on crime means

91

getting tough on black folks! That is the subliminal message that is really being invoked by politicians and that is why they want to keep as many black, white, Asian, Hispanic etc ex-felons away from the ballot box. If politicians are to scare people into voting for them in exchange for being offered a sense of protection, they will not be able to depend on the ex-felon's vote. As we dawn toward 2012 ex-felons are becoming the largest growing segment of our population in America. Ex-Felons are the new melting pot because felons are black, white, red and yellow. They are young and old. They are protestant and catholic. They are rich and poor. We will be a force to reckon with once we are able to come together and organize!

The greatest setup in American history is the history of America and its protection of the ballot-box. There is power in the ballot-box. Whoever controls the ballot-box in America will control America and the world. Hubert Blaylock (1973) was an American theorist who came up with the power-threat hypothesis. Blaylock hypothesis states that when majority populations feel threatened economically or politically whether the threat is real or perceived they will resort to any means necessary to stay in power. In reality that is exactly what happened to freed slaves during the

93

reconstruction era. When slaves were freed white folks begin to ride horses with sheets over their heads to scare/intimidate black folks from going to the voting polls. White folks knew then what they know now and that is if you give up the ballot box you give up your way of life to the new culture or minority population.

In America it is perfectly legal for unconvicted inmates to vote while they are in jail. All jails and prisons in the United States are supposed to provide absentee ballots to any inmate who has not been convicted of a felony so that they can vote. And for states like Maine even convicted felons are allowed to vote even if they are in prison. What is wrong with that picture? Maine is 99% white and mostly conservative. Why won't the states of Louisiana, Mississippi, Arkansas, Alabama and Georgia allow inmates to vote? I don't have to answer that question because every one of you reading this book knows the answer already. Chances are you will never hear the ten o'clock news or six o'clock news mention to unconvicted inmates that they have a right to vote and they can demand that right. If the jails deny them the right to vote they can sue them for violating their civil rights under the Civil Rights Bill of 1964. No police department or sheriff department wants to be charged with this. It can

95

cause the demise of a whole department. You become the 6 and 10 o'clock news and spread the word to others inmates about their rights.

Even more hypocritical is the fact that in many states ex-felons are not allowed to hold public office. The constitution is very clear in regards to no taxation without representation. How can you tax me and make me pay for a government that I am not allowed to take an active part in? I am hoping to witness a complete overhaul of the system in this regard. If people believe in you and trust you, I think that it should be their decision to decide if they want you in office or not. In America there are too many laws that prevent ex-felons from fully integrating back into society. Ex-felons walk around town with a scarlet letter on their chest and forehead everyday because America will never let you forget that you are a criminal. Yet we say that ex-felons have paid their debts to society. My question is that if we have paid our debt, why are we still paying? How much do we owe? Will we pay until the day we die? Folks do not realize how many barriers are placed in your path regardless of how long you have been off of paper. Some felons have been off of paper for thirty years. Never been arrested or in any trouble but they still have to put on applications that they were convicted of a felony and explain

97

their charge. I think that is very unfair. There should be a limit as to how long a person should have to answer that question and it should be enforced by state and federal law. The longer I live the more I associate the MARK of the BEAST with our DOC numbers. The only difference is that in the bible it says if you did not have the number you would not be able to eat, buy and would be killed. In America, if you have a Department of Corrections (DOC) number, once you are released from prison, it is hard to find work, which makes it hard to eat, and you certainly can't buy anything without money. Now there are some colleges that are running criminal background checks on students.

Chapter VII

Why Were/Are Drug Convictions The Only Crimes Used To Deny Federal and State Subsidies? Including Student Loans, Grants and Federal Housing.

It is time that we all start asking questions and demanding answers and if we don't like the answers do something about it. Why Are Mass Murders, Rapists, and Child Molesters Eligible to Receive Grants, Loans, Federal and State Subsidies, but Convicted Drug Users and Dealers are not? Make no mistake about it. The state legislators knew exactly what they were proposing when they decided to use drugs as the crime of choice to prevent minority offenders from receiving financial aid to obtain their college education. Why

99

drugs? Have you ever asked yourself this question? If the legislators wanted to be equitable, why would they use the crime that poor folks and black folks seem to commit most to deny access to financial aid? Drugs have been a part of the black experience since days of old. Drugs have been used by black folks for decades because drugs allow people to escape for a while. If you are lonely, drugs allow you to escape. If you are depressed, drugs allow you to escape. If you are broke, drugs allow you to escape. Additionally, drugs have been used as a way to earn income in the black community. Black men and women have long resorted to becoming street pharmacists, regardless of the risk they have encountered because they know and understand the great need for drugs that are present in black communities. I cannot write this chapter without listing some of the reasons that black folks use drugs. People with low self-esteem, poor morals, and those who are just simply stressed out resort to drugs for comfort when they are dealing with difficult times. Difficult times can include any of the following; when children are acting up, spouses are tripping, when in-laws are getting on your nerves, when folks at your job are tripping, when church folks make you upset, when relationships are on the rocks, and when bill collectors are calling and writing. All of the above plus hundreds of additional reasons allow us to justify our needs for drugs and alcohol.

If anybody should be granted financial aid it should be those brothers and sisters who have the mark as being ex-felons. Instead, they (legislators) have targeted the black drug dealer to make sure he or she does not receive financial aid. Forget the child rapist, let them get financial aid. Let the mass murders like Ted Bundy, Richard Ramirez and Jeffery Dahmer get financial aid but the street drug dealer cannot get financial aid. Who do you think they had in mind when they passed this law? Wake up and smell the coffee. Recently, they have changed the law and now the law says that if you are convicted of selling drugs while you are receiving financial aid, your financial aid can be suspended for 10 years. I have a serious problem with this. I don't see any laws saying that if you are a mass murderer, rapist, child molester, or white collar criminal and you are convicted of either of these crimes while you are receiving financial aid you will forfeit your financial aid for ten years. So again, I ask that you wake up and smell the coffee. Who do you think

they are really targeting with this law? Over 60% of African

Americans in prison are in there for drugs or drug related

charges. God will make away somehow! Which crime is

most heinous, murder, child molestation, raping or selling

weed or crack? Think about it! When the light comes it will

reveal everything!!!

Chapter VIII

The Black Church's Silence on Black Incarceration and Its Sin of Omission!

Where is the black church? What happened to the black

church? If I could rephrase the question I would like to ask

where are the black people? What happened to the black

people? What is the purpose of the church? Are we as the church doing all we can to help the people?

Have you not heard? Shall we continue in sin that grace may abound? No. God forbid. Where is the church? What is the purpose of the church in this era in which we have the largest and highest incarceration rate in the history of the world? Black folks are disproportionally locked up in every state in the United States. That means that our percentages in the prisons are more than our percentages in the populations. Where is the church? Let me be the first one to say that I believe that God is still in charge, but I also believe that the black church has become more concerned about image than effectiveness. We are more concern about political correctness than righteousness. Sometimes it is ok and within the rights of Christians to say to the world like the prophet Amos, let righteousness run down like a mighty stream. It is ok for the church to take a stand! But we are so conditioned to keep an immaculate image until we forget about the very people that we are supposed to be helping. What are the black church and its conventions doing to reduce disproportionate minority confinement? What are we doing to help prevent juveniles from ever coming into contact with the juvenile justice system? What are we doing in a proactive manner to prevent our children from going to prison and jail? I want the world to know that jail is not a rite of passage for manhood in the black community. Some people have asked the question, has the church let the people down or have the people let the church down? God has been very good to our race in America. We have come a long way! As Jesse Jackson said we have come from the outhouse to the White House! Going to jail is not a rite of passage for our young black men. We don't have to go to jail or prison to be a man! I am asking each man to reach one young black youth and mentor him or her. Each one reaches one – that is the convict code! You know the system! Steer these young men down the right path. Going to jail don't mean that you are hard! Getting a good education and avoiding jail and prison means that you are smart!!! Making the dean's list and being on the national honor society means that your likelihood of making it in life is much more pronounced.

Once again I ask where is the church? Every black church in America should have at least three programs: an educational program to help their members learn how to read, have tutorials services, help members of the community get their GEDs and have at least five weekends in which we help our parishioners and the community enroll in college and complete their financial aid. Every black church should have social assistance programs which should include assistance with social security, disability, Medicare, Medicaid, summer feeding programs, utility assistances, jobs, and any other assistance needed to help the poor and deserving populations. Finally, every black church in America should have medical programs in which black folks should be able to be tested for high blood pressure, sugar diabetes, HIV, cholesterol, mammograms, pap smears, prostate cancer, colon cancer, and all other illnesses that plague the black community. I love mega-churches and hope to one day develop our church to the mega church status but I believe that the church should serve the people. We need churches to join ranks and open community development corporations, credit unions, and housing projects. If we are going to spend money why not spend it with and among ourselves? Where are the black folks? We know what it is going to take to turn the tide. The question is, are we willing to take the initial steps to do it? The church has to step up, speak up, act up and show up!!!

Chapter IX

The Biggest Rip-Off Of the 21st Century – Ex-Felon Re-Entry Programs, Who's really being helped "The Ex-Cons or the New Cons"?

When we evaluate the programs and see where the money going, we see who is really being helped? Some folks are standing in line to get money to help the ex-convicts, but in the end they help themselves! Earmarks, Earmarks and Earmarks!!!

The congress has appropriated millions of dollars to every state to help train ex-felons. Of the millions and billions of dollars that have been spent, I have never seen a report that explicitly details how many ex-felons were trained and how many have gotten jobs. Black folks don't have a problem working on jobs; we have a problem finding jobs. If we want to help ex-felons, we need to spend this money on creating jobs not training for jobs. The government in my opinion is just up to their old tricks. The congress is just up to their old tricks. The new Cons are just up to their old tricks. Are we really trying to help the poor and outcast members of our society or are we just helping ourselves? That is the question. We all know that even if you train people and they don't have a job to go to, we have not done them any good. There is a strong undercurrent running in America and it is called greed! In this particular case, ex-felons are being exploited! Many of these folks do not care whether these ex-felons get jobs or not, they only care about getting their pay checks. I see all kinds of grey areas in this legislation. If these programs are beneficial to the taxpayers why haven't we seen the reports to support them? After all the money used to support these initiatives come from taxpayers like you and I. We must hold our government accountable! Who's zooming who!

Chapter X

2011 and Beyond – The New Ex-Convict Empowerment Era – Why We Can No Longer Be Ignored!

I am not Nostradamus or Ms. Cleo but I am predicting the dawn of a new class, a special interest group, a new minority and that is the ex-felon. Remember whoever controls the ballot box will control the power and decision making in America. As we dawn toward a new day in 2012, we must realize that the ex-con can no longer be ignored. There are approximately 25 - 30 million ex-felons in the United States.

Ex-felons outnumber a lot of groups and others special interest groups. Ex-felons are becoming the new largest minority group in America. Every year in America over 1 million people are convicted of a felony. Every year these numbers continue to rise. If you check the history of America, England used America as a dumping ground for their criminals. When criminals were kicked out of England, America and Australia were the places that they were sent. Despite this, we know that every year new laws are enacted and the more laws you enact, the wider the net and the more people you will arrest for breaking laws.

I would like to one day appeal to ex felons to unite and organize. It is time we stand up and be accounted for. There are 330 million people in America and if 25-30 million are ex-felons we can control the ballot box if we unite. I want ex-felons to think outside of the box. If democrats or republicans are more sensitive to our needs as ex-felons then that is the party that we should support. No longer are we just going to support the democrats. I love the democrats and I have been a democrat all of my life but I now vote based on the issues not just based on my party. The ex-felon programs are in my opinion a big rip off. We as taxpayers are paying many folks rents and sending their children to college on our hard earned and spent taxes. Wake up people!

Chapter XI

The Top 100 Companies in the U.S. and their Policies on Hiring Ex-Felons

In the fall of 2006, I embarked on a long, tedious journey trying to survey the largest 100 companies in the U.S. My research produced startling results. Companies did not want to disclose information about their hiring practices as it relates to ex-felons, and I know why. There consensus was in my opinion that if they did not hire ex-felons then why should ex-felons buy their products? In America THERE ARE APPROXIMATELY 25-30 million ex-felons. There are roughly 330 million people in America and of those 1 out of every 40 people that you meet in the U.S.A. are felons. We will never be able to level the playing fields as long as companies who have no reason not to hire ex-felons will not, and we do not take the opportunity to confront businesses that refuse to hire us. Additionally, we must question any and all legislation that reduces the power and influence of ex-felons in the U.S. As time permit, I will certainly follow up on this research.

Chapter XII

Why Ex-Convicts and Their Families Should Boycott Any Businesses That Do Not Hire Ex-Felons. "They Don't Hire, We Don't Buy" The Ex-Felon's Pledge!

I am encouraging all ex-felons to boycott any businesses that do not hire ex-felons. If a company says that they do not hire ex-felons then I am asking that we boycott their product or service. If they don't hire we don't buy! It is just as simple as that! Once we have paid our debt to society, society should release us from the debt! We can no longer be punished for life for mistakes that we have already paid for. Now is the time. If you affect a man's back pocket, you WILL get his attention! That is a fact. "No hire/No buy"! Tell your family if they don't hire, we don't buy! Money is the greatest motivator! I am not saying child rapist should work in daycare centers but I am saying that if you are qualified for a job and you have paid your debt to society employers should give you a chance to work. No man or woman who has paid their debt to society should be punished for the rest of their lives for crimes that they committed once upon a time. When will we stop this madness? If God cast our sins into the lake of forgiveness never to rise again, why should we have to be punished for life for crimes that we have committed and spent time in prison, jail or on probation for?

Chapter XIII

Strategically Designing Unsound, Ineffective, Disorganized Communities Prone to Violence, Crime, Welfare, and Hopelessness. Welcome To Black America!

White folks have strategically designed the black neighborhoods to be unproductive. They do not put banks, colleges, stores, movie theaters etc in the neighborhood. But you can always find a plethora of pawn shops, nightclubs, and gambling parlors. Why is this? Why do they allow places of vice to be located in our neighborhoods? The more important question is why do we as African Americans allow other races to place shady businesses in our communities? Many of these business owners are like leaches. They come into our communities with the pawn shops, liquor stores, payday loans, night clubs, etc and suck our money out of our communities and at the end of the night they go home to the suburbs in their quite communities. They have in reality raped up. They take from us and do not give anything to our communities in return. Our children do not attend the schools that their children attend, they do not get the medical services that they get, they don't attend the same synagogues and churches that we attend but they take our moneys to their hoods. We don't own anything when it is all said and done. The white man's and other men's ice is always colder than our ice. We must start supporting one another. A house divided against itself cannot stand! We've got to unite!! If we don't unite our communities will continue to unravel, deteriorate, remain ineffective, disorganized, be prone to violence, crime, welfare and hopelessness! When will we wake up and join hands and work together? We can no longer allow other people to regulate how we will live out our legacies. We must unite!!

If there is one thing that really makes me upset it is the Uncle Tom Negro who is so afraid to challenge the status quo that he takes sides with the enemy. The passive resistor who is so ingrained in white culture, light skin, material wealth and status that he cannot see injustice. There are many black folks in America who can make something happen positively for their communities but they are constantly bombarded with negativities from the Uncle Tom. Martin Luther King said that no man can ride your back

119

unless you are bent over! Stand up! Speak up, look up and be a man!

If you are scared, stay out of the civil rights business. If you are not willing to go all the way, don't start the race or the journey! If your heart is not in it, get out of the civil rights business. But if you know that you deserve more than you have and you want more than you've got, get up and do something about it!!

My only regret is that I only have one live to give for my people. I love everything about this life. I want to see our race be respected more and the only way that will happen is if we get more education, and we respect one another and work together. We don't realize the power that we would possess if we worked together. We have been bamboozled, tricked and had for a long time but now is the time that we wake up!

Chapter XIV

A Black President in the White House – "Amazing Grace How Sweet The Sound" That Saved A Wretch Like Me, I Once Was Lost But Now I Am Found, Was Blind But Now I See!

When God says yes, nothing else matters! No one really believed that President Obama, really had a chance to win the democratic nomination and it is certain that very few folks believed that he would win the election for President, but if God be for you, who can be against you? Since President Obama has been in the white house he has faced all kinds of oppositions. The republicans have regrouped, the Tea Party has become enraged and many of our white brothers and sisters have just become uncivilized in their actions and propaganda toward our president and the liberals in America. It seems that the white race has come together to achieve one goal and that goal is to make sure that President Obama is not re-elected in 2014. This story is yet to unfold! Some of these conservative would be willing to vote for the devil instead of re-electing this black man! They don't care who run, I believe that they would even elect Charles Manson just to get a black man out of the White house. Surprisingly, it is not the middle and upper class whites who harbor this animosity, but it is the poor, uneducated or undereducated whites who exhibit these attitudes toward the president and the liberal democrats. They just want to get this black man out of the White House. I would not put any

122

money on it. Many people are disgruntled with America and many of the young white, blacks, Asians, and Hispanics believe that President Obama is doing a great job. They did not come out in massive numbers during the recent election which resulted in the republicans taking the house but, you can bet your last money on the fact that they will come out in record numbers for the presidential election in 2013. President Obama will be re-elected!! Not because he is black, but because he is a very good president. He is respected all over the world. He is advocating for equality and equal treatment for all people. God is good!

Chapter XV

Utopia, Why Is It So Hard For Us to Understand That There Is Enough of Resources On Earth To Feed, Cloth And Provide Shelter For All Of Us? There Is Enough For All Of Us!

When will we realize that there are enough resources on earth for everybody to be happy? We fight, rant and rave over resources but in reality, there are enough of resources for all of us to have everything that we need. In America we throw away enough food each day to feed people in many third world countries. If we just transported 1/5 of the bath water that we use in America, we could eradicate thirst and malaria in third world countries. We really don't know how good we've got it in America. We have enough wood and bricks on earth to build everyone on earth a nice house. We have enough food and water on earth to make sure that no one goes to bed hungry or thirsty. We have enough cotton, polyester, silk and rayon to make sure that everyone is clothed on earth. Why is it we cannot realize that we can have global peace and harmony and protect the future of our children and grandchildren? In the words of that great man in California who made the quote of the century, "Can't we all just get alone"? America let's take the lead in doing what is right? Let's give!!!

Chapter XVI

The Solutions to America's Crime and Prison Problem

There are certain things that I will recommend to America for consideration if we are serious about reducing our prison populations and reducing crime. Some of the solutions include;

- Legalization of Marijuana: we all know that the only reason that weed is not legalized is because it is a cash crop and all you need is a light bulb, dirt, seeds and water and weed will grow anywhere. The government knows that alcohol is more harmful and kills way more people than weed but because they cannot tax weed properly, they have not legalized it. Prior to the 1938 Marijuana Tax Act, marijuana was not illegal. I agree with Bob Marley, we ought to legalize it!

- Put more money into education at the front end. Mandatory Quality Education for all students

126

beginning at age 2. No Exceptions! Let's get serious, we need to give each child a fair chance to succeed and the only way we can do this is to let them begin school at the same time. Many minority kids do not go to school until they are four years old.

- Release all state, federal and county prisoners being held for drug possessions in which the amount did not exceed 5 grams. Come on people who are these people hurting? We will spend 30,000 per year on an inmate whose only crime is that they had an addiction. These people are not a threat to society, they are a threat to weed and crack. Locking these people up for five years @ a rate of 30,000 per year is ridiculous. This is tax payer's money we are using to pay for these people's addictions.

- Declare a moratorium on traffic tickets and traffic warrants and forgive all persons who have outstanding citations and warrants and allow them to have their licenses reinstated within 90 days. This would be mind boggling. Do we realize how many students and citizens do not have their driver's licenses because of traffic tickets and warrants? That is why I know that the majority is trying to set us up with this new ID law. They are saying people will not be able to vote if they do not have an ID. You and I both know that this is

128

aimed at black folks and poor folks. If you have not paid child support you cannot get a license. If you don't have a job you cannot pay child support! Come on People! This is a set up. Remember the Power Threat Theory Hubert Blalock (1973).

- Allow all persons on probation, parole and those who are awaiting trial in county jails to be able to vote. No exceptions! This is the law in several jurisdictions. If a person is awaiting trial and they have not been convicted of a felony, there are no laws in America that prevents or disqualifies them from voting. Jail inmates you must raise your voices and demand your right to vote!

129

- Allow all ex-felons to run for political offices at the city, county, state, and federal levels. No exceptions! Once a man or woman is released from jail, there should be no law, at the state or federal level that should prevent them from running for public office. If we enact such laws, we are not supporting democracy, which is government of the people, by the people and for the people. If people have confidence in ex-felons, they should be able to exercise their rights to choose the best candidate. Come on People!

- Abolish mandatory minimum sentencing. We must allow Judges to look at pre-sentence investigation reports and give them discretion to

130

pronounce sentences based on the facts of the case and the individual characteristics of the offender.

- Abolish the three strikes laws and all laws that enhance punishment for offenders. It is a fact that most criminals begin to age out of the criminal process once they reach the age of 40. There is no need to continue to lock up older non-violent offenders for extensive periods of time when they are no threat to the general public and the research suggest that criminal activities decline in the latter years for non-violent offenders.

- Create more community alternative sentencing for moral offenders such as prostitutes, addicts, and alcoholics. These people are not a danger to

131

citizens; they are a danger to themselves. Placing them in prison for 3-5 years do not address the root problems that they are dealing with. We have to treat their problems, addictions and stressors that they are dealing with. We can no longer sweep their problems under the rug. We have to face the problems affecting this sub-section of our population.

- Release all non-violent drug offenders. These people are not a threat to society; frankly, they just want to get high! Help these people find work, legalize marijuana, tax the marijuana and the incarceration rate is reduced by 20%. Use the tax revenue from the marijuana sales to invest in the early education of our citizens. We can eradicate poverty and a substantial amount of illiteracy and poverty by implementing this model.

- As I sit in my hotel room on this day 11-9-11, Maine just rejected the voter ID bill, which would require all voters to present an ID before they could vote. The implementation of this bill will set America back 100 years and would be liken unto the poll tax of the 1890's. We know who this bill is aimed at. What a shame! Come on People!!!!

Food for Thought!

Karl Marx and Frederich Engels talk about the bourgeoisie and proletariat, the wealthy business owners and the poor line workers. Have you ever thought about the fact that the assembly line workers actually make the cars for GM, Ford, Chrysler etc, but the CEO's make the millions, yet they do not build any automobiles? What is preventing the line workers from buying their own assembly line and manufacturing their own cars and adequately distributing the wealth? The answer, Capital aka money! Many corporations dangle the carrot before their employees because we are creatures of habit. If we make 50,000 a years we live like we make 50,000 a year. If we make 17,500 a year we live like we make 17,500 a year. Employers only pay us enough to pay our mortgages, utilities, car notes, insurance and have a little left for recreation but will never allow us to save enough to buy our assembly lines! Think about it! This is food for thought!

RIP; Heavy D-The Overweight Lover 11-8-11

    Smoking Joe Frazier – 11-7-11

President Barack Obama- I love you brother, keep pressing toward the mark. I know what kind of hell you are facing and I am 100% committed to making sure you are re-elected in 2012. May God continue to bless you, your family and the presidency!

The greatest legacy that a man can leave is a legacy in which his family, friends and others knew that he did stand for SOMETHING. (Tracy Andrus 2011)

9 7 8 1 4 5 1 5 5 0 6 3 4